CREATE YOUR OWN LIFE'S STORY

THE SIMPLE WAY TO RECORD
YOUR PERSONAL HISTORY

Glen Walker

BRISTOL PUBLISHING ENTERPRISES
San Leandro, California

Printed in the United States of America.

ISBN 1-55867-087-4
Library of Congress Catalog Card Number 93-79322

Cover design by Frank Paredes
Cover photography by John Benson

HOW TO USE
CREATE YOUR OWN LIFE'S STORY

This book has been developed to make it easy and interesting for you to create a permanent written record of your personal history.

Here's how to do it.

1. Fill in the blanks for each statement that is applicable to you. For longer sections, you may want to use scratch paper for a first draft of your thoughts.

2. Disregard (and discard) any pages of the book that are not applicable to you (for example, military service or divorce).

3. Following significant dates, you will find a statement saying, "This year (19__) was the year that ..." Turn to the section at the back of the book for facts about each year from 1905 through 1992. Use these (or other events you remember) to complete the statements about what was happening during significant years of your life.

4. Pages are perforated and three-hole punched. As you complete the pages, tear them out and insert them into any standard three-ring binder (not supplied). A suggestion: Try one of the attractive three-ring binder photo albums; use some of the photo album pages to insert photos at appropriate places in your book.

5. If you prefer, you can leave the pages in this book. Tear out and discard pages that do not apply to you.

6. There are extra lined pages behind the *New Products* section. Copy these pages to add additional material in any section. Use blank sheets to paste in photos, letters, favorite poems and other material. This is, after all, *Your Own Life's Story*. Use your imagination to make it memorable.

INTRODUCTION

What follows are facts and reflections about my life. In general, I can say that my life has been

_____

_____

_____

_____

_____

I have tried to follow these principles and guidelines in my life:

_____

_____

_____

_____

_____

_____

_____

_____

_____

_____

_____

_____

_____

REMEMBRANCE

I would like to be remembered as a person who

_____

_____

_____

_____

_____

_____

_____

_____

_____

_____

_____

_____

_____

_____

_____

_____

_____

_____

_____

_____

_____

_____

_____

_____

_____

MOST MEMORABLE YEAR

I would say that the most memorable year of my life has been _____

That was the year in which I _____

_____

_____

_____

_____

_____

_____

_____

_____

_____

_____

_____

_____

_____

_____

_____

_____

Of course, other things were happening in that year. I remember that
this was the year (19__) that _____

_____

_____

_____

_____

_____

_____

MY CHILDHOOD

I was born in_____ on_____, 19___.

This was the year (19__) that_____

_____

_____

_____

_____

_____

My full name is _____

My parents chose that name because_____

_____

_____

_____

This is what I know about my birth:_____

_____

_____

_____

_____

_____

In my growing up years, we lived in_____

_____

_____

This place was known for _____

_____

_____

_____

One of my favorite memories of this place is _____

_____

_____

_____

Things I liked most about growing up there: _____

_____

_____

_____

_____

Things I did *not* like about growing up there:_____

_____

_____

_____

_____

My parents told me that as a baby, I was _____

_____

_____

_____

_____

My earliest memory of this time is_____

_____

_____

_____

_____

My favorite toys as a child were_____

_____

_____

_____

_____

_____

My best friend in these early years was _____

_____

Here are some of the games my friend and I enjoyed playing:

_____

_____

_____

_____

_____

Sometimes I was naughty. Here are some of the times I can remember getting in trouble:_____

_____

_____

_____

_____

_____

My favorite books as a child were _____

_____

_____

_____

_____

_____

The first movie I can remember seeing was _____

_____

My favorite movies and movie stars as a child were _____

_____

_____

_____

_____

_____

I had chores to do as a child. My chores began when I was about___years old. I was supposed to _____

_____

_____

_____

When I did not do my chores, my punishment was_____

_____

_____

_____

Some children get an allowance. This is what my parents did:_____

_____

_____

_____

When I behaved and did my chores, I would sometimes get a special treat. My favorite treat was _____

_____

My best "grown-up" friend in my childhood was _____

_____

I liked my "grown-up" friend because _____

_____

_____

_____

My favorite holiday as a child was_____because_____

_____

I think the big differences between the lives of children today and the lives of children of my generation are_____

_____

_____

_____

_____

_____

_____

MY FATHER

My father's name: _____

He was born in_____on_____, 19__.

This was the year (19__) that_____

_____

_____

_____

_____

When I was young, this is what my father did for a living: _____

_____

_____

Later, his work was _____

_____

_____

When he wasn't working, my father liked to_____

_____

_____

_____

One of my favorite memories of my father is the time he _____

_____

_____

_____

My father taught me many things. Here are some of the most important
things that I can remember: _____

_____

_____

_____

_____

_____

I think the things my father was proudest of included _____

_____

_____

_____

_____

My father could have a temper. Things that made him angry:

_____

_____

_____

_____

My father's favorite:

Song: _____

Book: _____

Vacation place:_____

_____

Holiday:_____

Hobby: _____

_____

My father enjoyed playing the following sports:

_____

_____

_____

_____

_____

My father's favorite sports team was _____

_____

He followed their games by _____

_____

_____

_____

_____

The first car I can remember that my father drove was _____

_____

_____

_____

I think the cost of the car was about $_____

Special drives we used to take included _____

_____

_____

_____

_____

_____

_____

My father's best friend during my childhood years was_____

_____

_____

Together, they used to enjoy _____

_____

_____

_____

_____

_____

My mother said that the best quality about my father was _____

_____

_____

_____

My mother's biggest complaint about my father was that he _____

_____

_____

_____

There were many things my father did that I liked very much and have come to appreciate over the years. These include

_____

_____

_____

_____

_____

There were also things my father did that I did not like. For instance,

_____

_____

_____

_____

The biggest argument I ever had with my father was about _____

_____

_____

_____

_____

Some further notes about my father:

_____

_____

_____

_____

_____

_____

_____

_____

_____

_____

_____

MY MOTHER

My mother's name:_____

She was born on_____, 19__ in _____

This was the year (19__) that _____

_____

_____

_____

_____

When I was young, my mother's work was _____

_____

_____

Later, my mother's work included _____

_____

_____

When she wasn't working, my mother liked to _____

_____

_____

_____

One of my favorite memories of my mother is the time she _____

_____

_____

_____

My mother taught me many things. Here are some of the most important
things that I can remember:_____

_____

_____

_____

_____

_____

I think the things my mother was proudest of included _____

_____

_____

_____

_____

My mother could have a temper. Things that made her angry:

_____

_____

_____

My mother's favorite:

Song:_____

Book:_____

Vacation place:_____

_____

Holiday:_____

Hobby:_____

_____

My mother's favorite recreation was_____

_____

_____

_____

_____

_____

She liked to do this by _____

_____

_____

_____

_____

My mother had mixed feelings about the family car. She felt that

_____

_____

My mother's best friend during my childhood years was

_____

_____

Together, they liked to_____

_____

_____

_____

_____

_____

My mother especially enjoyed doing these things with her family:

_____

_____

_____

_____

_____

_____

My father said that my mother's best qualities included

_____

_____

_____

My father's biggest complaint about my mother was that she _____

_____

_____

_____

I remember the things my mother did that I liked very much. For instance,

_____

_____

_____

_____

_____

_____

There were also things that my mother did that I did not like. These included_____

_____

_____

_____

_____

The biggest quarrel I ever had with my mother was about_____

_____

_____

_____

_____

The result of that quarrel was that_____

_____

_____

Some further notes about my mother:

_____

_____

_____

_____

_____

_____

_____

_____

MY FAMILY TREE

Here is information about my family and its history.

My mother's name:_____

Maiden name:_____

Date of birth: _____

Place of birth:_____

My father's name:_____

Date of birth:_____

Place of birth:_____

Their children, dates of birth and places of birth:

_____

_____

_____

_____

_____

_____

Their grandchildren, dates of birth and places of birth:

_____

_____

_____

_____

_____

_____

_____

_____

My mother's family

Her mother's name: _____

Date of birth: _____

Place of birth:_____

Her father's name: _____

Date of birth: _____

Place of birth:_____

My mother's brothers and sisters:

_____

_____

_____

My father's family

His mother's name:_____

Date of birth: _____

Place of birth:_____

His father's name:_____

Date of birth: _____

Place of birth:_____

My father's brother and sisters:

_____

_____

_____

My mother's ancestors came here originally from

_____

_____

My father's ancestors came here originally from

_____

_____

In addition to those I have listed, other relatives and ancestors I have been told about over the years include

_____

_____

_____

_____

_____

_____

_____

_____

My parents or grandparents told me these stories about our family:

_____

_____

_____

_____

_____

_____

_____

_____

_____

_____

_____

_____

_____

_____

_____

Our family has roots in these countries:

_____

_____

_____

_____

The first members of my family to come to the United States were

_____

_____

_____

_____

They left the country of their birth because

_____

_____

_____

_____

When they arrived in this country, I am told that they had to do the following in order to survive:

_____

_____

_____

_____

Other notes about my ancestors:

_____

_____

_____

_____

_____

HEALTH AND FAMILY

I want to record information about our family's health and some of the medical problems we have faced over the years.

Health problems I am experiencing now include

_____

_____

_____

_____

Health problems I experienced in the past include

_____

_____

_____

_____

The most important things I have done to stay healthy include

_____

_____

If I had known then what I know now about health, I would not have

_____

_____

The most serious health problem I have faced in my life was

_____

_____

Here's how this condition was treated:

_____

_____

_____

Here's what I know about the age and cause of death of members of our family:

Name	Relation	Cause of Death	Age
_____	_____	_____	_____
_____	_____	_____	_____
_____	_____	_____	_____
_____	_____	_____	_____
_____	_____	_____	_____
_____	_____	_____	_____
_____	_____	_____	_____
_____	_____	_____	_____
_____	_____	_____	_____
_____	_____	_____	_____

Our family has a history of health problems in the following areas:

_____

_____

_____

_____

_____

Other notes about the health of members of our family:

_____

_____

_____

_____

_____

_____

_____

_____

GRAMMAR SCHOOL

I first attended school in 19__.

The name of the school was _____

It was located in _____

Many families move from one neighborhood to another, or from one town to another, and children change schools. This is what happened to me: _____

_____

_____

_____

_____

_____

This is how I got to school and back: _____

_____

_____

There was one teacher I especially remember, because _____

_____

_____

_____

Other teachers I can remember:

_____

_____

_____

_____

_____

_____

_____

_____

_____

_____

_____

_____

I can remember this about the school buildings and the furniture:

_____

_____

_____

_____

In those days, this is how we dressed for school: _____

_____

_____

My favorite subjects in grammar school were _____

_____

_____

_____

_____

_____

I really disliked these subjects: _____

_____

_____

_____

There were some special events during my grammar school experience:

_____

_____

_____

_____

_____

_____

These are some of my memories of summer vacations: _____

_____

_____

_____

_____

_____

MEMORABLE TIMES BEFORE I WAS 20

There are so many memorable times and events, both happy and sad, proud and not so proud. My most vivid memory of things that occurred before I reached the age of 20 is

The year:_____ The time that_____

_____

_____

_____

_____

That was the year (19__) that _____

_____

_____

_____

_____

Other memorable events in my years before reaching age 20:

The year:_____ The time that_____

_____

_____

_____

_____

The year:_____ The time that_____

_____

_____

_____

The year:_____ The time that_____

_____

_____

_____

I acquired a nickname or two in these young years, including

_____

I got my nicknames because_____

_____

_____

My parents said that as a teenager, I was_____

_____

_____

_____

_____

Actually I think that as a teenager, I was _____

_____

_____

_____

_____

The biggest difference between teenagers then and teenagers today is

_____

_____

_____

_____

_____

The birthday I remember best during these years was when I reached
the age of ___. It was memorable because _____

_____

_____

_____

_____

_____

_____

_____

HIGH SCHOOL

My high school was _____

It was located in_____

I attended high school from _____ to_____

I was graduated from high school in _____

That was the year (19__) that_____

_____

_____

_____

My favorite subject in high school was_____

_____

because _____

_____

The subject I liked least in high school was_____

_____

because_____

_____

My proudest achievement in high school was

_____

_____

_____

_____

_____

_____

My most embarrassing time in high school was the time that

_____

_____

My closest friends in high school were_____

_____

_____

_____

High school friends I stayed in touch with in later years include

_____

_____

After class each day, I usually spent my time

_____

_____

_____

_____

In high school, I got my highest grades in these subjects:

_____

_____

_____

_____

I got my lowest grades in these subjects:

_____

_____

_____

_____

Some of my favorites during my high school years:

Song: _____

Dance: _____

Movie star: _____

Movies:_____

_____

Sports heroes:_____

My favorite sports were_____

_____

My sports activities in high school included _____

_____

_____

_____

The most popular styles for boys and girls then were_____

_____

Besides classes and studying, I was involved in these activities during
high school _____

_____

_____

_____

_____

_____

_____

_____

I debated several careers during high school. Among the career choices I
considered at one time or another were_____

_____

_____

_____

_____

The teacher I most remember from high school was_____

_____

because_____

_____

_____

Here is how I usually did my homework in high school: _____

_____

_____

_____

_____

Things that were going on nationally and locally that worried us the most during high school were: _____

_____

_____

_____

If I had my high school years to live over again, I would do the following differently:

_____

_____

_____

_____

_____

_____

_____

_____

Some other memories of my high school years:

_____

_____

_____

_____

_____

_____

_____

_____

_____

MEMORABLE TIMES BETWEEN THE AGES OF 20 AND 29

Life is an adventure in one's 20s. My most vivid memory of events that occurred between the time I was 20 and 29 years old is

The year:_____ The time that_____

_____

_____

_____

_____

That was the year (19__) that_____

_____

_____

_____

_____

Other memorable events in my years between 20 and 29:

The year:_____ The time that_____

_____

_____

_____

The year:_____ The time that_____

_____

_____

_____

The year:_____ The time that_____

_____

_____

_____

I left home and began living on my own when I was __ years old. Let me tell you about the first place I lived after leaving home:

_____

_____

_____

_____

Other places that I lived when I was in my 20s included

_____

_____

_____

_____

Young men and young women usually met each other by

_____

_____

_____

_____

A typical date for people in their 20s then generally involved

_____

_____

_____

_____

The kind of date I most enjoyed in my 20s was to

_____

_____

_____

_____

When I was in my 20s, the things that were going on nationally and locally that most concerned me included

_____

_____

_____

_____

COLLEGE OR UNIVERSITY

My college/university training was at _____

_____

I attended from _____ to_____

These were the years (19__ to 19__) that_____

_____

_____

_____

_____

I earned the following certificates or degrees:

_____

_____

My major subject during these years was _____

Minor subjects I also studied included _____

_____

_____

_____

The subject I liked least was_____

because _____

_____

_____

The subject I liked most was _____

because _____

_____

_____

My proudest achievement in college was _____

_____

_____

My most embarrassing time was _____

_____

_____

College friends I stayed in touch with in later years include

_____

_____

_____

After class each day, I usually spent my time _____

_____

_____

_____

I got my highest grades in these subjects: _____

_____

_____

I got my lowest grades in these subjects:_____

_____

_____

Some of my favorites during my college years:

Song:_____

Movie:_____

TV show:_____

Dance: _____

Movie star: _____

My favorite politician_____

because_____

_____

_____

For recreation, I most enjoyed _____

_____

_____

_____

The most difficult time I experienced during my college years was

_____

_____

_____

This is how my education was financed: _____

_____

_____

_____

_____

I got to and from classes each day in the following manner:

_____

_____

The way we dressed for class in those days was_____

_____

_____

_____

My sports activities included_____

_____

_____

_____

As for fraternities and sororities, my own experience was_____

_____

_____

_____

The teacher or professor I most remember is _____
because_____

_____

_____

_____

This is how I usually studied: _____

_____

_____

_____

If I had my university years to live over again, I would do the following differently:_____

_____

_____

_____

_____

_____

_____

Some other memories of my college years:

_____

_____

_____

_____

_____

_____

_____

_____

_____

_____

_____

_____

_____

_____

_____

_____

_____

_____

POST-GRADUATE EDUCATION

My post-graduate education was at _____

_____

I attended from _____ to _____

These were the years (19__ to 19__) that _____

_____

_____

_____

_____

I earned the following certificates or degrees: _____

_____

My major subject during these years was _____

_____

Other subjects I studied included_____

_____

My proudest achievement during this period was _____

_____

_____

_____

Special projects that were part of my post-graduate work:

_____

_____

_____

A post-graduate degree was important to me because

_____

_____

_____

_____

_____

_____

The major people I was able to study under or who otherwise influenced me were _____

_____

I held the following jobs while I was doing my post-graduate work:

_____

_____

_____

My closest friend in graduate school was_____

If I were to advise a young person today about whether to go to graduate school, I would say

_____

_____

_____

_____

_____

_____

If I had it to do over again myself, I might approach graduate school differently. I would

_____

_____

Major concerns nationally and locally while I was in graduate school:

_____

_____

_____

_____

MARRIAGE

I want to describe my wedding to _____

It took place on _____ , 19___ , in_____ .

That was the year (19__) that_____

_____

_____

_____

_____

We were married in _____

_____

_____

The ceremony was performed by _____

_____

Those attending the ceremony included _____

_____

_____

_____

This is how we met: _____

_____

_____

_____

Our courtship had lasted about_____ before we decided to marry.

I remember this about the marriage proposal:_____

_____

_____

_____

This was our parents' reaction to our plans:_____

_____

_____

_____

For our honeymoon, we went to _____

_____

_____

_____

_____

Before the marriage, my work was _____

_____

_____

After the marriage, my work was _____

_____

_____

This was the work my new spouse did before and after the wedding:

_____

_____

_____

_____

Our first home was at _____

_____

_____

I would describe our first home as_____

_____

_____

_____

_____

We lived there from_____ to_____. My favorite
memory of this time is _____

_____

_____

_____

_____

_____

_____

My favorite memories of those early marriage years include

_____

_____

_____

_____

_____

_____

_____

_____

_____

The biggest adjustment I had to make after our marriage was _____

_____

_____

_____

_____

_____

The biggest adjustment that _____ had to make after our marriage was _____

_____

_____

_____

_____

I remember some of our first arguments: _____

_____

_____

_____

In my judgment, the secret to a happy marriage is _____

_____

_____

_____

One of the most interesting trips we took together was _____

_____

_____

_____

Here are some other dates and events that are among the highlights of our life together.

19__. _____

_____

19__. _____

_____

19__. _____

_____

19__. _____

_____

19__. _____

_____

To make the record complete, here are other dates and facts I want to add about my married life:

_____

_____

_____

_____

_____

_____

THE CHILDREN

Our children, and their dates of birth:

_____

_____

_____

_____

_____

_____

Every child's name is special. In our case, here is why we selected the names we did:

_____

_____

_____

_____

_____

_____

_____

Here are the places we lived, and the names of the schools our children attended, during the growing-up years:

_____

_____

_____

_____

_____

_____

_____

_____

_____

_____

_____

Every child has special qualities. Here are descriptions of the special qualities of each of our children:

_____

_____

_____

_____

_____

_____

_____

_____

I suppose every parent has favorite stories about the children. In my case, those stories would have to include

_____

_____

_____

_____

_____

_____

_____

_____

_____

_____

_____

_____

_____

_____

_____

_____

Of course, every parent has a "proudest moment." In my case, those moments are

_____

_____

_____

_____

_____

_____

_____

_____

_____

_____

And there also are moments of great worry in raising a family. In my case, those times include

The time that _____

_____

_____

The time that _____

_____

_____

The time that _____

_____

_____

The time that _____

_____

_____

Here is a "status report" on each member of our family at the time of this writing:

_____

_____

_____

_____

_____

_____

_____

_____

_____

_____

_____

_____

_____

_____

_____

_____

_____

_____

_____

_____

_____

_____

_____

_____

_____

_____

DIVORCE

I was divorced from_____on_____, 19__ .

We had been married for_____ years.

Many things contributed to the divorce. I think the problem that finally made divorce necessary was _____

_____

_____

_____

_____

_____

My own views about divorce, in general, are_____

_____

_____

_____

_____

_____

The most difficult adjustment to make after the divorce was_____

_____

_____

_____

_____

If I knew then what I know now about this marriage and divorce, I might have done things differently. I might have _____

_____

_____

_____

_____

Attitudes about divorce have changed during my lifetime. The change that I have observed is _____

_____

_____

_____

If a friend or relative were contemplating divorce, and asked my advice, I would say _____

_____

_____

_____

_____

_____

_____

My life changed after the divorce. Among other things, I found myself

_____

_____

_____

_____

_____

Other thoughts about divorce:

_____

_____

_____

_____

_____

_____

_____

MILITARY SERVICE

Let me tell you about my time in military service.

I entered the _____ on _____ , 19___ ,
serving for_____years.

During this time, I served in the following locations:

_____

_____

_____

_____

My duties in the service were devoted primarily to

_____

_____

_____

_____

_____

_____

I held these ranks during my time in the service:

_____

_____

_____

_____

I received these citations and commendations:

_____

_____

_____

_____

Here are memories of people I met and what they were like during my
military service:

_____

_____

_____

_____

_____

_____

_____

If I were to describe my feelings about my military service, I would say

_____

_____

_____

_____

_____

_____

_____

_____

_____

_____

_____

_____

_____

_____

_____

TIMES OF WAR AND HISTORY

During my lifetime, I can recall this country being at war or involved in wartime conflicts on the following occasions:

_____

_____

_____

_____

_____

Here is what was happening in my life during each of those periods:

_____

_____

_____

_____

_____

There were other times of great turmoil in this country. I have vivid memories of what I was doing at the time I learned that:

_____

At the time, I was _____

_____

When I learned about_____

I was_____

_____

_____

When I learned about_____

I was_____

_____

_____

Members of my family who have served in wars or other great national emergencies include

_____ , who was _____

_____

_____

_____ , who was _____

_____

_____

_____ , who was _____

_____

_____

Other memories I have about the wars and other significant events of history during my lifetime:

_____

_____

_____

_____

_____

_____

_____

_____

_____

_____

_____

_____

_____

_____

_____

_____

POLITICS

I want to share my views about politics.
The President I most admired was _____
because he _____

_____

_____

_____

_____

_____

The President I least admired was _____
because he _____

_____

_____

_____

_____

Another politician I liked the most was _____
because he/she _____

_____

_____

_____

_____

I belong to the _____ Party for these reasons:

_____

_____

_____

_____

_____

_____

_____

I may not have always agreed with the candidates or the views of that party. Some of my areas of disagreement include

_____

_____

_____

_____

Major political issues come and go. Here are some of the major political issues that have occurred during my lifetime and my views of them.

Issue: _____

My views:_____

_____

_____

Issue: _____

My views:_____

_____

_____

Issue: _____

My views:_____

_____

_____

Issue: _____

My views:_____

_____

_____

Of course, I may change my mind about some of these issues. One issue about which I felt strongly, and then later changed my point of view was

_____

_____

_____

_____

_____

_____

_____

MY FAITH

If I were to try to describe my feelings about religion, I would say that

_____

_____

_____

_____

_____

As to my congregation, I am a member of_____

_____

_____

_____

Services I have performed in connection with my religion include

_____

_____

_____

_____

_____

The religious upbringing of my parents:

Mother: _____

_____

_____

Father: _____

_____

_____

My earliest memory of my religious training is _____

_____

_____

_____

My feeling about introducing children to religious ideals is

_____

_____

If I were to try to describe God, I would say that God is

_____

_____

_____

_____

Here are other reflections I want to share about religion:

_____

_____

_____

_____

_____

_____

_____

_____

_____

_____

_____

_____

_____

_____

_____

_____

FRIENDSHIPS

True friendships are rare. My best friends over the years have included

_____

_____

_____

_____

One of the fondest memories I have of a time with a friend was when

_____

_____

_____

_____

_____

_____

_____

One of the finest things a friend ever did for me was the time that

_____

_____

_____

_____

_____

_____

_____

Friends have arguments, too. I can recall one argument I had with my friend_____. This is what it was about:

_____

_____

_____

One of the funniest things that happened to me involving a friend was
the time that _____

_____

_____

_____

_____

_____

_____

The things I have most enjoyed doing with my friends include

_____

_____

_____

_____

_____

_____

_____

To me, a friend is one who _____

_____

_____

_____

_____

_____

_____

_____

_____

_____

_____

MEMORABLE TIMES BETWEEN THE AGES OF 30 AND 39

There is a different sense of direction in one's 30s. My most vivid memory of events that occurred between the time I was 30 and 39 years of age is

The year:_____ The time that_____

_____

_____

_____

_____

That was the year (19__) that_____

_____

_____

_____

_____

Other memorable events in my years between 30 and 39:

The year:_____ The time that_____

_____

_____

_____

_____

The year:_____ The time that_____

_____

_____

_____

The year:_____ The time that_____

_____

_____

_____

I remember that when I reached age 30, I felt as though

_____

_____

_____

My work changed when I was in my 30s. Here are some of the changes
that took place:_____

_____

_____

_____

_____

_____

There were major changes in my life at home between the time I was 30
and 39. Among the most important changes:

_____

_____

_____

_____

_____

_____

_____

_____

Times of greatest joy during these years included

_____

_____

_____

Times of greatest sadness during these years included

_____

_____

_____

_____

My ambition in life when I was in my 30s was

_____

_____

_____

_____

_____

A great deal happened between the time I was 30 (19__) and the time I was 39 (19__). Among other things, these were the years that

_____

_____

_____

_____

_____

_____

_____

_____

_____

_____

_____

_____

_____

I had many friends during my 30s. Here are the names of some of them and what they were doing then and now:

_____

_____

_____

_____

_____

_____

_____

Achievements of which I am proudest during this time:

_____

_____

_____

Some of my favorites when I was in my 30s:

Singing artist:_____

Movie:_____

Movie star: _____

Television show:_____

Television star:_____

Author:_____

Book:_____

Sports team: _____

Sports star: _____

Events that occurred nationally and locally that most excited me when I was in my 30s:

_____

_____

_____

_____

Events that occurred nationally and locally that most troubled me when I was in my 30s:

_____

_____

_____

_____

The biggest difference between becoming 30 when I did and becoming 30 today is

_____

_____

_____

_____

WORK AND MONEY

My first job was _____

_____

_____

_____

The year was _____. This is how much I earned:_____

Later jobs, when they occurred and how much I earned:

_____

_____

_____

_____

_____

_____

_____

_____

_____

_____

_____

_____

_____

_____

_____

_____

_____

_____

_____

_____

Today, my occupation is_____

_____

_____

_____

I first began this work in _____.

This was the year (19__) that _____

_____

_____

My proudest accomplishments in my work include:

_____

_____

_____

_____

_____

_____

_____

_____

_____

Am I happy that I chose this work? Let me put it this way:

_____

_____

_____

_____

_____

_____

_____

_____

Bosses from hell? Well, maybe one or two. Among the ones I remember best, and what made then cantankerous, were

_____

_____

_____

_____

_____

But I was fortunate to have some great bosses. Among the ones I remember best, and what made them great, were

_____

_____

_____

_____

_____

Have I thought seriously about other work? You bet! Here are some of the other jobs I thought would be interesting:

_____

_____

_____

_____

_____

Looking back, the changes I might have made to make my work and my career more rewarding would include

_____

_____

_____

_____

_____

My advice to young people trying to decide on a job or career today is

_____

_____

_____

_____

There have been times in my life when I had very little money. Let me tell you when those times occurred and how I managed:

_____

_____

_____

_____

_____

_____

_____

This is how I have managed and invested money over the years:

_____

_____

_____

_____

_____

_____

In my opinion, this is the way to invest your money soundly:

_____

_____

_____

_____

_____

_____

_____

_____

MEMORABLE TIMES BETWEEN THE AGES OF 40 AND 49

They say that life begins at 40. My most vivid memory of events that occurred between the time I was 40 and 49 years old is

The year:_____ The time that_____

_____

_____

_____

_____

That was the year (19__) that_____

_____

_____

_____

_____

Other memorable events in my years between 40 and 49:

The year:_____ The time that_____

_____

_____

_____

_____

The year:_____ The time that_____

_____

_____

_____

_____

The year:_____ The time that_____

_____

_____

_____

_____

One's 40th birthday is a big one. I remember that when I reached 40 I felt as though

_____

_____

_____

Here's how I remember observing my 40th birthday:

_____

_____

_____

There were many changes in my personal life when I was in my 40s. Among the most important changes:

_____

_____

_____

_____

_____

There were changes in my work as well. Among them:

_____

_____

_____

_____

_____

Times of greatest joy during these years included

_____

_____

Times of greatest sadness during these years included

_____

_____

TRAVEL

In all my travels, the place that I enjoyed most was _____

because_____

_____

_____

_____

_____

A place I have not been that I would really like to visit is_____

because_____

_____

_____

_____

The method of travel I most enjoy or would like to try is _____

_____

_____

_____

The biggest pleasure for me in traveling is _____

_____

_____

_____

The worst thing about traveling is _____

_____

_____

The most dreadful trip I ever took was the time _____

_____

_____

The first childhood trip I can remember: _____

_____

_____

_____

When I travel, I like to stay at _____

_____

_____

A couple of vacation trips that I recommend highly are

_____

_____

_____

A couple of vacation trips that I would never recommend include

_____

_____

_____

My travel plans for the future include

_____

_____

_____

_____

Other reflections on vacations I have taken and places I have been:

_____

_____

_____

_____

_____

_____

_____

_____

_____

_____

_____

_____

_____

_____

MEMORABLE TIMES AFTER
I REACHED THE AGE OF 50

Does a person change dramatically after half a century? I don't think so.
My most vivid memory of events that occurred after I reached age 50 is

The year:_____ The time that_____

_____

_____

_____

_____

That was the year (19__) that_____

_____

_____

_____

_____

Other memorable events in my years after reaching age 50:

The year:_____ The time that_____

_____

_____

_____

_____

The year:_____ The time that_____

_____

_____

_____

_____

The year:_____ The time that_____

_____

_____

_____

Here's how I remember observing my 50th birthday:

_____

_____

I remember thinking on my 50th birthday that_____

_____

_____

_____

There were many changes in my personal life when I was in my 50s.
Among the most important changes; _____

_____

_____

_____

_____

There were changes also in my work. Among them:

_____

_____

_____

_____

While I may admit to being older than 50, I feel inside as though my age
is ___. However, my body tells me I'm no longer quite so young. For
example, I no longer _____

_____

_____

_____

Times of greatest joy when I was in my 50s:_____

_____

_____

_____

I reached age 50 in 19__. That was the year that _____

_____

_____

_____

GOLDEN YEARS

No matter what they tell you, the so-called "golden years" are in fact

_____

_____

_____

_____

As I write this today, I am ___ years old. Generally speaking, I feel

_____

_____

_____

There are many good things about growing older. Here are some of them:

_____

_____

_____

There are things I used to worry about that no longer seem so important to me. For example, I feel a bit more mellow about _____

_____

_____

_____

However, I still feel strongly about many things. Among them:

_____

_____

_____

The things that please me the most about young people today are

_____

_____

_____

The things that irritate me most about young people today are

_____

_____

_____

The things that worry me the most about young people today are

_____

_____

Times of greatest joy for me in recent years include _____

_____

_____

_____

Times of sadness for me in recent years include _____

_____

_____

_____

Other important events that have affected me and those I care about in
recent years include _____

_____

_____

_____

The activities I most enjoy these days are _____

_____

_____

_____

_____

Activities I can quite happily do without include _____

_____

_____

_____

_____

Right now, I am really looking forward to _____

_____

_____

_____

_____

RETIREMENT

I (plan to/did) retire upon reaching the age of ____
because _____

_____

_____

_____

My plans for retirement include _____

_____

_____

_____

_____

_____

_____

The retirement activities that interest me the most are _____

_____

_____

_____

_____

_____

I think that the biggest adjustment one has to make in retirement is ____

_____

_____

_____

The biggest worry in retirement is _____

_____

_____

_____

The biggest pleasure for me in retirement is or will be _____

_____

_____

Where and how I live is important to me in retirement. My plans are to

_____

_____

_____

_____

_____

The one thing I never want to lose in my retirement years is my _____

_____

_____

I hope that in my retirement years my family and friends will _____

_____

_____

My advice for those who are thinking about retirement is _____

_____

_____

_____

_____

_____

_____

_____

_____

HOBBIES AND AMUSEMENTS

When I am not busy with my daily work and have some time to myself, I enjoy_____

_____

_____

_____

_____

_____

When I go out for the evening, my favorite activities are _____

_____

_____

_____

_____

I have belonged to or continue to belong to the following organizations:

_____

_____

_____

_____

_____

These are the positions I held or some special projects I was involved in with these organizations:_____

_____

_____

_____

_____

_____

_____

_____

Many people collect items of interest. These are the things I have collected over the years: _____

_____

_____

_____

_____

_____

Special classes I have taken or talents I have developed:_____

_____

_____

_____

_____

_____

_____

_____

Other hobbies or interests of mine:_____

_____

_____

_____

_____

_____

_____

_____

_____

_____

_____

_____

_____

NEW PRODUCTS AND INVENTIONS DURING MY LIFETIME

Since I was a child, there have been many new products and inventions that have changed the way people live. Here are some of them, and the approximate times in my life that they became available.

Foods:

_____

_____

_____

_____

_____

Household appliances:

_____

_____

_____

_____

_____

Transportation:

_____

_____

_____

_____

Tools:

_____

_____

_____

_____

Business machines:

_____

_____

_____

_____

Materials:

_____

_____

_____

_____

Communication:

_____

_____

_____

_____

Medicine:

_____

_____

_____

_____

Other new products or inventions:

_____

_____

_____

_____

_____

THAT WAS THE YEAR THAT...

1905
Orville Wright made a 30-minute flight at Daytona, Florida. Greta Garbo was born. Franklin and Eleanore Roosevelt were married in New York. Pavlov showed that dogs would salivate at the sound of a bell. The Rotary Club was founded.

1906
An earthquake and fires destroyed much of San Francisco, killing 500. Automatic carriage return for typewriters was invented.

1907
Suffragettes stormed Parliament in England seeking the right to vote. The Second Hague Peace Conference adopted rules of war. Laurence Olivier was born. The Ziegfield follies opened in New York.

1908
James Stewart was born. An earthquake killed 150,000 in Italy and Sicily. The New York Board of Education banned whipping in schools. The first Model T auto was produced, selling for $850. General Motors was organized. William Howard Taft was elected President.

1909
Admiral Peary raised the flag at the North Pole. Katherine Hepburn was born. Sigmund Freud visited the U.S. to explain his theory of psychoanalysis.

1910
The Boy Scouts of America was founded. The NAACP was organized. Florence Nightingale died at 90. Author Mark Twain died.

1911
Ronald Reagan was born. Sun Yat-sen was named president of the new Chinese Republic. The Supreme Court dissolved the Standard Oil Company. Marie Curie won the Nobel Prize for the discovery of radium. Chevrolet Motor Company was formed.

1912
More than 1,500 passengers died when the Titanic hit an iceberg and sank. Woodrow Wilson was elected President. War was declared in the Balkans.

1913
The Sixteenth Amendment (income tax) was adopted. New York's Grand Central Terminal opened. Richard Nixon was born. Charlie Chaplin made his first film appearance. Henry Ford opened his automobile assembly line.

1914
The Panama Canal opened. Austrian Archduke Ferdinand was assassinated, launching World War I. The Clayton Antitrust Act gave unions the right to strike. E.R. Burroughs' *Tarzan of the Apes* was published.

1915
U.S. banks loaned $500 million to France and Britain. The British ship Lusitania was sunk with the loss of 128 American lives. German zeppelins bombed London. Albert Einstein published his theory of relativity. Alexander Graham Bell made the first telephone call.

1916
President Wilson was re-elected on an anti-war platform. British troops put down the Easter Rebellion in Ireland. Ford Motor Company reduced the price of a new car to $250. British and French forces captured 22,000 Germans in the Battle of the Somme. The U.S. bought the Virgin Islands from Denmark for $25 million.

1917
The U.S. entered the war in Europe to "make the world safe for democracy." Lenin returned to Russia following the abdication of Czar Nicholas II, and the Bolsheviks seized power.

1918
Germany signed an armistice and World War I ended. The U.S. recognized Czechoslovakia as a nation.

1919
The first commercial flight was introduced between Paris and London. The League of Nations was created. Jack Dempsey became heavyweight champion. The Eighteenth Amendment (prohibition) was adopted. Race riots in Chicago left 30 dead, 500 injured.

1920
The first Agatha Christie mystery was published. Pitcher Babe Ruth was sold to the New York Yankees for $125,000. Women won the right to vote in the U.S. "Shoeless" Joe Jackson and other Chicago White Sox players were indicted for conspiring to fix the World Series. Warren Harding was elected President.

1921
The Ku Klux Klan began a revival. German war liability was fixed at 132 billion gold marks, beginning massive inflation. Race riots in Tulsa left 85 dead. Tenor Enrico Caruso died. Rudolph Valentino's *The Sheik* opened in New York.

1922
The first issue of *The Reader's Digest* was published. The Irish Free State was proclaimed. Mussolini's Fascist Party took over the government in Italy. Irving Berlin introduced *April Showers*.

1923
Adolph Hitler was sentenced to five years in prison. French and Belgian troops occupied the Ruhr when Germany fell behind in reparations. Bessie Smith recorded *Down-Hearted Blues*. President Harding died of a stroke. Marathon dancing became popular.

1924
Stalin became Soviet dictator, ruling until 1953. Lenin died at 54. Leopold and Loeb confessed to the thrill killing of Bobby Franks. Calvin Coolidge was elected President. American Indians were made citizens.

1925

Wyoming elected the first woman governor. Chiang Kai-shek became leader of China. William Jennings Bryan died a few days after winning the Scopes evolution trial in Tennessee. Hitler published *Mein Kampf*. Charleston was the latest dance craze.

1926

Marines occupied Nicaragua during a revolt. Marilyn Monroe was born. Rudolph Valentino died at 31. Gene Tunney defeated Jack Dempsey for the heavyweight boxing crown.

1927

The German economy collapsed. Clara Bow starred in the movie *It*. Charles Lindbergh flew the Atlantic in the "Spirit of St. Louis." Babe Ruth hit his 60th home run. Popular songs: *My Blue Heaven, Ol' Man River*. Al Jolson starred in *The Jazz Singer*, a talking movie.

1928

Penicillin was discovered. Shirley Temple was born. Amelia Earhart flew across the Atlantic. Mortimer Mouse became Mickey Mouse in the cartoon *Steamboat Willie*. Herbert Hoover was elected President.

1929

Vatican City was established. Seven gangsters were slain in the Valentine's Day massacre in Chicago. The stock market crashed, ushering in the Great Depression. Hemingway's *A Farewell to Arms* was published.

1930

Nazis gained power in German elections. New York City began installing traffic lights. Prohibition had its 10th anniversary. Popular song: *I Got Rhythm*. Marlene Dietrich starred in *Blue Angel*.

1931

Japan occupied Manchuria. Notre Dame coach Knute Rockne died in a plane crash. The Empire State Building, world's tallest at 86 stories, opened. Al Capone was sentenced to 11 years in prison for tax evasion. Popular song: *Mood Indigo*.

1932

Veterans marched on Washington, D.C. Charles Lindbergh's baby was kidnapped and later found dead. Franklin Delano Roosevelt was elected President. The jobless rate reached 11 million. Johnny Weissmuller starred in *Tarzan*.

1933

Hitler became chancellor of Germany. The U.S. recognized the U.S.S.R. Congress created the Civilian Conservation Corps to ease unemployment. Roosevelt ordered banks closed for seven days. Prohibition ended with the repeal of the Eighteenth Amendment.

1934

The Dionne quintuplets were born in Canada. Max Baer became the world heavyweight champion. Bank robbers Bonnie and Clyde were killed by police. Fred Astaire and Ginger Rogers starred in *The Gay Divorcee*.

1935

Mussolini's troops invaded Ethiopia. Elvis Presley was born. The Social Security Act was signed into law. The National Labor Relations Act was passed to protect unions. Humorist Will Rogers died in a plane crash. A DC-3, carrying 21 passengers, made its first flight.

1936

Germany produced the Volkswagen automobile. War began between China and Japan. The Boulder Dam was completed. Jesse Owens won four gold medals at the Berlin Olympics. Roosevelt was elected to a second term. Popular song: *Pennies From Heaven*.

1937

Amelia Earhart was lost in flight. Nylon was patented. Japan sank the U.S. gunboat Panay. The Golden Gate Bridge opened in San Francisco. Joe Louis became heavyweight champion, defeating James Braddock. The Duke and Duchess of Windsor were married in France.

1938

Hitler's Germany took over Austria. Joe Louis defeated Max Schmeling in the first round. The Fair Labor Standards Act set the minimum wage at 40 cents an hour. Irving Berlin's *God Bless America* was introduced by Kate Smith. A nationwide scare was caused by Orson Welles's broadcast of *The War of the Worlds*.

1939

Einstein wrote Roosevelt about the feasibility of an atomic bomb. Britain and France declared war on Germany after the invasion of Poland. The U.S. proclaimed its neutrality. Popular movies: *Wizard of Oz, Gone With the Wind, Mr. Smith Goes to Washington*.

1940

Winston Churchill became prime minister of Britain. The U.S. sent 50 destroyers to Britain. Finland surrendered to Russia. Allied troops escaped at Dunkirk. France fell to Germany. Japan allied itself with Germany and Italy. German planes bombed Britain.

1941

Japan attacked Pearl Harbor, and the U.S. declared war on Axis powers. The Manhattan Project began atom bomb research. Movie *Citizen Kane* opened. The British Royal Navy sank the German warship Bismarck. Germany invaded Russia and was turned back at Moscow. Hong Kong surrendered to Japan.

1942

The Declaration of United Nations was signed. The U.S. put 100,000 Japanese in detention camps. Nazi leaders met in Berlin to plan "the final solution," the annihilation of Jews. Singapore and Philippines surrendered to Japan. General Doolittle's bombers hit Tokyo. The U.S. Navy defeated Japanese at Midway.

1943

Rationing of canned goods, coffee and sugar began in the U.S. Prices and wages were frozen to prevent inflation. Guadalcanal was liberated by American troops. Federal troops curbed race riots in Detroit. Income tax withholding began. Mussolini was deposed after the Allies invaded Italy.

1944

D-Day began as Allied forces landed in Normandy and liberated Paris. The G.I. Bill of Rights was enacted. Roosevelt won a fourth term, with Harry S. Truman as Vice President. MacArthur's troops took the Philippines.

1945

Roosevelt died. Truman became President. Germany surrendered. Hiroshima and Nagasaki were destroyed by atomic bombs. Japan surrendered. The United Nations was formed in San Francisco.

1946

Churchill warned of Russian "Iron Curtain." U.S. gave the Philippines their independence. Nehru was appointed head of India's government. Xerox copying was introduced. W.C. Fields died. Popular song: *Zip-a-dee-doo-dah*. Nine Nazi leaders were hanged for war crimes after Nuremberg war trial.

1947

Marshall Plan was proposed for Europe's recovery. India and Pakistan were granted independence by Britain. *Howdy Doody* was a popular TV program. The film industry was investigated by the House Un-American Activities Committee. Jackie Robinson broke the color barrier and became a Brooklyn Dodger.

1948

Communists seized power in Czechoslovakia. Mahatma Gandhi was assassinated in India. U.S. and Britain airlifted supplies to blockaded Berlin. Joe Louis defeated Jersey Joe Walcott. Truman defeated Thomas Dewey for President. The nation of Israel was proclaimed. A new Cadillac cost $3,000. The Kinsey Report was published.

1949

The annual cost of educating a public school child was $206, compared to $88 in 1940. Chinese Communists established the People's Republic. NATO was formed. Popular song: *Rudolph the Red-Nosed Reindeer*. Russia announced it had the atomic bomb. The Comet, the first jetliner, was introduced.

1950

The New York Yankees swept the World Series in four games against Philadelphia. U.N. forces landed at Inchon, turning the tide of the Korean war. The Army seized U.S. railroads to prevent a strike. Althea Gibson became the first black to compete in U.S. tennis championship. The government issued a guide on home shelters against atom bomb attack.

1951

The Twenty-Second Amendment was passed, limiting the President to two terms. Truman relieved MacArthur of command in Korea. J.D. Salinger published *The Catcher in the Rye*. Truce was declared in Korea. Sugar Ray Robinson became middleweight champion.

1952

Sam Snead won the Masters Gold Tournament, earning $4,000. Dwight D. Eisenhower was elected President. Christine Jorgenson had a sex change operation. Popular song: *Your Cheatin' Heart*. Auto air conditioning was introduced. *High Noon* was named the best film of 1952.

1953
Lucille Ball signed an $8 million deal to continue *I Love Lucy* through 1955. New York Yankees won their fifth World Series. Soviet tanks crushed an uprising in East Berlin. Ernest Hemingway won the Pulitzer Prize for *The Old Man and the Sea*. Julius and Ethel Rosenberg were executed. Joseph Stalin died.

1954
Eisenhower signed a bill inserting the words *under God* into the Pledge of Allegiance. Senator McCarthy was censured by the Senate. The Supreme Court outlawed school segregation. Robert Bannister became the first to break the four-minute mile. Communists defeated the French at Dien Bien Phu. The Boeing 707 jet was introduced.

1955
The population of New York City reached 8 million. AFL and CIO were merged. Disneyland opened in California. Brooklyn Dodgers won the World Series. Film star James Dean died in a car accident. Popular song: *Davy Crockett*. The YMCA voted to admit women.

1956
Blacks boycotted city buses in Montgomery. Marilyn Monroe married Arthur Miller. Eisenhower and Nixon were reelected. A revolt in Hungary was crushed by the Soviets. U.N. cease-fire was declared in Suez Canal attack by British, French and Israelis.

1957
The average American's schooling was 11.8 years, with 9% completing college. European nations formed the Common Market. Humphrey Bogart died of throat cancer. Russia launched Sputnik, the first satellite. Eisenhower sent troops to Little Rock to integrate schools. The musical *West Side Story* opened.

1958
The Packard auto was discontinued. U.S. launched the Explorer I satellite. Thalidomide caused thousands of birth defects in Europe. Popular song: *Catch a Falling Star*. Van Cliburn won Soviet piano competition. The movie *Gigi* opened.

1959
Fidel Castro took over Cuba. Alaska became the 49th state, Hawaii the 50th. The U.S. sent two monkeys into orbit. Mayor Daley's salary in Chicago was raised from $25,000 to $35,000.

1960
John F. Kennedy was elected President after TV debates with Nixon. Clark Gable died. Nikita Khrushchev banged his shoe on the table at the U.N. Nazi Adolf Eichmann was captured by Israelis. Gary Powers' U-2 spy plane was shot down over the Soviet Union. Popular song and dance: *Let's Do the Twist*.

1961
Castro defeated an invasion at the Bay of Pigs. Russia exploded a hydrogen bomb. Yuri Gagarin of Russia became the first man in space, followed by Alan Shepard of the U.S. Actor Gary Cooper died. Communists constructed the Berlin Wall.

1962

John Glenn became the first American to orbit the earth. Kennedy forced the Soviets to retreat in Cuban missile crisis. France gave independence to Algeria. James Meredith became the first black at the University of Mississippi. Marilyn Monroe was found dead of a drug overdose.

1963

Kennedy made his "Ich bin ein Berliner" speech at the Berlin Wall. The Supreme Court outlawed the recitation of the Lord's Prayer in schools. Pope John XXIII died and Pope Paul VI was crowned. Martin Luther King told followers in Washington, "I have a dream." President Kennedy was assassinated in Dallas. Lyndon Johnson became President.

1964

The Beatles appeared on the Ed Sullivan TV show. Ford introduced the Mustang. Three civil rights workers were murdered in Mississippi. President Johnson signed the Civil Rights Act. Johnson defeated Goldwater for President. Martin Luther King received the Nobel Peace Prize. Brezhnev replaced Khrushchev in Russia.

1965

Race riots erupted in Watts. Johnson signed the Medicare bill. Ontario power failure blacked out eight northeastern states. Martin Luther King led 25,000 on a freedom march in Alabama. Cassius Clay (Muhammad Ali) defeated Sonny Liston for the heavyweight championship. More than 184,000 U.S. troops were in Vietnam.

1966

The first heart transplant was performed. President Johnson visited troops in Vietnam. The miniskirt became popular. Walt Disney died. California elected Ronald Reagan governor. A sniper at the University of Texas tower killed 12. Frank Sinatra wed Mia Farrow.

1967

Three astronauts were killed in Apollo I fire. Muhammad Ali lost his title for refusing the draft. Israel won the Six-Day War. Red China tested a hydrogen bomb. Popular film: *The Graduate*. Thurgood Marshall became the first black on the Supreme Court.

1968

President Johnson, beset by Vietnam losses, announced he would not seek reelection. Martin Luther King was assassinated in Memphis. Senator Robert Kennedy was assassinated in Los Angeles. Richard Nixon was elected President. Russia invaded Czechoslovakia to crush a revolt.

1969

Astronaut Neil Armstrong became the first man on the moon. Nearly 400,000 attended the Woodstock music festival. Mary Jo Kopechne drowned at Chappaquiddick in a car driven by Senator Edward Kennedy. The New York Mets won the World Series.

1970

Four students were killed by the National Guard at Kent State protest on Vietnam. Rhodesia became a Republic. The Postal Service became an independent agency. Popular song: *Bridge Over Troubled Water*. Janis Joplin died of a drug overdose.

1971

The U.N. admitted Communist China. School busing to achieve desegregation was upheld by the Supreme Court. The voting age was reduced from 21 to 18. The London Bridge was moved to Arizona. Louis Armstrong died. The Supreme Court permitted publication of the Pentagon Papers on Vietnam.

1972

Bobby Fischer won the world chess championship. Seven persons were indicted for breaking into Democratic headquarters at Watergate. Britain took direct rule of Northern Ireland. Eleven Israeli athletes were killed by Arab terrorists at the Munich Olympics. Nixon defeated George McGovern for President.

1973

The military draft ended. Nixon's secretary admitted erasing 18 minutes of Watergate tapes. Israelis pushed back a Yom Kippur attack by Arabs. Great Britain entered the Common Market. Spiro Agnew resigned as Vice President after a tax evasion charge.

1974

Patty Hearst joined her kidnappers as an outlaw. President Nixon resigned. Gerald Ford succeeded him. Muhammad Ali regained the heavyweight title. Jimmy Connors won the U.S. Open. The Heimlich maneuver was introduced.

1975

Americans left Vietnam and Saigon surrendered to the Communists. Popular film: *Jaws*. Casey Stengel died. William Douglas retired from the Supreme Court. The U.S. population reached 13.6 million.

1976

Jimmy Carter was elected President. Legionnaire's disease killed 29 in Philadelphia. The U.S. celebrated its 200th anniversary. Viking I and Viking II landed on Mars and sent back pictures. Popular films: *Rocky, Network*. Swine flu vaccine was distributed nationally.

1977

President Carter pardoned most draft evaders. Elvis Presley died at 42. The movie *Star Wars* introduced R2D2. Two 747 jumbo jets collided in the Canary Islands, killing 574. An estimated 80 million watched *Roots* on TV.

1978

Egypt's Sadat and Israel's Begin met with President Carter at Camp David. Pope John Paul I died one month after his election. The first test-tube baby was born in London. California voters passed the Proposition 13 "tax revolt" measure. Rev. Jim Jones and 900 followers died in a mass murder-suicide in Jamestown, Guyana.

1979

Ayatollah Khomeini ousted the Shah of Iran. Iran took 90 hostages at the American Embassy. Margaret Thatcher became prime minister in Great Britain. John Wayne died. Mother Teresa won the Nobel Peace Prize. Sandinista rebels took over Nicaragua. Jane Byrne became Chicago's first woman mayor.

1980

Ronald Reagan was elected President. Philadelphia won the World Series. Former Beatle John Lennon was killed by a fan. The Moscow Olympics was boycotted because of the invasion of Afghanistan. Jimmy Durante died.

1981

The disease AIDS was identified. President Reagan was wounded in an assassination attempt. Sandra Day O'Connor became the first woman on the Supreme Court. Iran released the American hostages. Reagan fired striking air traffic controllers. Dan Rather replaced Walter Cronkite on CBS News.IBM stepped up marketing of its "personal computer" for home and office use.

1982

The Equal Rights Amendment failed. Barney Clark received the first artificial heart. Eight persons died in Tylenol poisonings. Princess Grace died in an auto accident. Popular movie: *E.T.* Britain defeated Argentina forces in the Falkland Islands.

1983

Poland's Walesa won the Nobel Peace Prize. Chicago elected its first black mayor. Soviets shot down a Korean airliner, killing 269. The U.S. invaded the Caribbean island of Grenada. A Beirut bomb killed more than 200 Marines. The Brooklyn Bridge was 100 years old.

1984

Reagan and Bush defeated Mondale and Ferraro. More than 2,000 were killed by a gas leak in Bhopal. Indira Gandhi was slain in New Delhi. Mary Lou Retton starred at the Los Angeles Olympics. The PG-13 rating was introduced for movies. Miss America resigned after posing for nude photos.

1985

A new Coca Cola was introduced, causing protests. Gorbachev became the Soviet leader. San Francisco won the Super Bowl. Boris Becker won at Wimbledon. The wreck of the Titanic was found. An earthquake hit Mexico city. Rock Hudson died of AIDS. Terrorists killed 18 in airport attacks in Rome and Vienna.

1986

The space shuttle Challenger exploded, killing seven. Russia acknowledged a nuclear power accident at Chernobyl. The White House admitted the sale of arms to Iran. Clint Eastwood was elected mayor of Carmel, Califonia. Marcos fled the Philippines, and Aquina became president.

1987

The U.S. and Russia agreed to destroy medium-range missiles. Jim Bakker resigned his ministry in a sex scandal. The U.S. budget reached a trillion dollars. The Dow dropped 508 points in a Wall Street crash. Congress began the Iran-Contra hearings. Popular movie: *Fatal Attraction.*

1988

George Bush was elected President. Russia withdrew its troops from Afghanistan. Massive drought plagued much of the U.S. The last Playboy Club closed in Michigan. The video game Nintendo was introduced. A bomb destroyed Pan Am Flight 103, killing 270. Steffi Graf won the tennis Grand Slam at age 19.

1989

Five thousand protesters were killed in China's Tiananmen Square. Japan's Hirohito died at 87. President Bush declared drugs Public Enemy No. 1. The worst earthquake since 1906 rocked the San Francisco area. Hungary, Poland, Czechoslovakia and Romania installed non-Communist governments. The U.S. invaded Panama, ousting Noriega.

1990

East Germany and West Germany were reunited. The Berlin Wall came down. Iraq invaded Kuwait. The U.S. and other nations began a massive troop buildup against Iraq. Cincinnati defeated Oakland in the World Series.

1991

Kuwait was liberated in the "Gulf War," a 28-nation action led by U.S. against Iraq. Pan American World Airways filed for bankruptcy. Clarence Thomas was the second black person appointed to the Supreme Court.

1992

Gov. Bill Clinton of Arkansas was elected the 42nd President. Following the Rodney King verdict, 52 persons died in the Los Angeles riots. U.S. Marines landed in Somalia in an effort to provide humanitarian relief.